The Rock Book

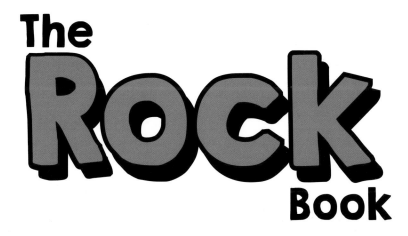

Pamela Chanko

Brought to you by the editors of

Children's Press®
An imprint of Scholastic Inc.

How to Read This Book

This book is for kids and grown-ups to read together—side by side.

A  means it's the kid's turn to read.

A grown-up can read the rest.

Simple text for kids who are learning to read

Harder text—that builds knowledge and vocabulary—for grown-ups to read aloud

This is a rock.

This is a rock.

Some rocks start to form deep inside Earth, where the rock is so hot it melts! This hot, melted rock is called **magma**. Sometimes magma comes out to Earth's surface. When magma cools, it gets hard again. It becomes **igneous** rock.

Granite is an igneous rock.

These are also igneous rocks.

pumice   basalt

When magma comes out of a volcano, it's called lava.

Some rocks form when wind, water, and ice break big rocks into tiny pieces, called sediment. The sediment goes into lakes and oceans. It piles up in layers. The layers press together to make **sedimentary** rock.

This is sedimentary rock. Can you see the layers?

6

7

Nonfiction text features like labels and captions

Bright photos to talk about

2

Table of Contents

The Wave is a sandstone rock formation in Arizona.
Sandstone is sedimentary rock.

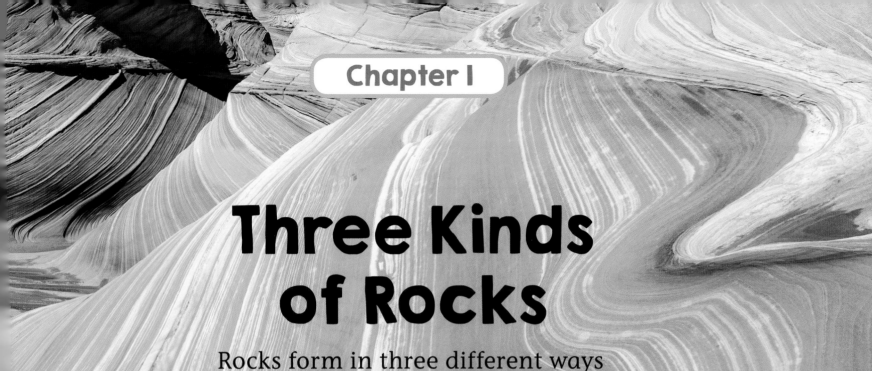

Three Kinds of Rocks

Rocks form in three different ways to make three kinds of rocks.

igneous

sedimentary

metamorphic

This is a rock.

Some rocks start to form deep inside Earth, where the rock is so hot it melts! This hot, melted rock is called **magma**. Sometimes magma comes out to Earth's surface. When magma cools, it gets hard again. It becomes **igneous** rock.

Granite is an igneous rock.

When magma comes out o a volcano, it's called lav

These are also igneous rocks.

pumice

basalt

6

This is a rock.

Some rocks form when wind, water, and ice eak big rocks into tiny pieces, called sediment. e sediment goes into lakes and oceans. It piles in layers. The layers press together to make dimentary rock.

This is sedimentary rock. Can you see the layers?

This is a rock.

Some rocks start as one type of rock and then turn into another! They are formed inside Earth, where they get heated and squeezed until they change. They are called **metamorphic** rocks.

Sedimentary Rocks	Metamorphic Rocks
sandstone	quartzite
limestone	marble

becomes

becomes

Lapis lazuli is a metamorphic rock.

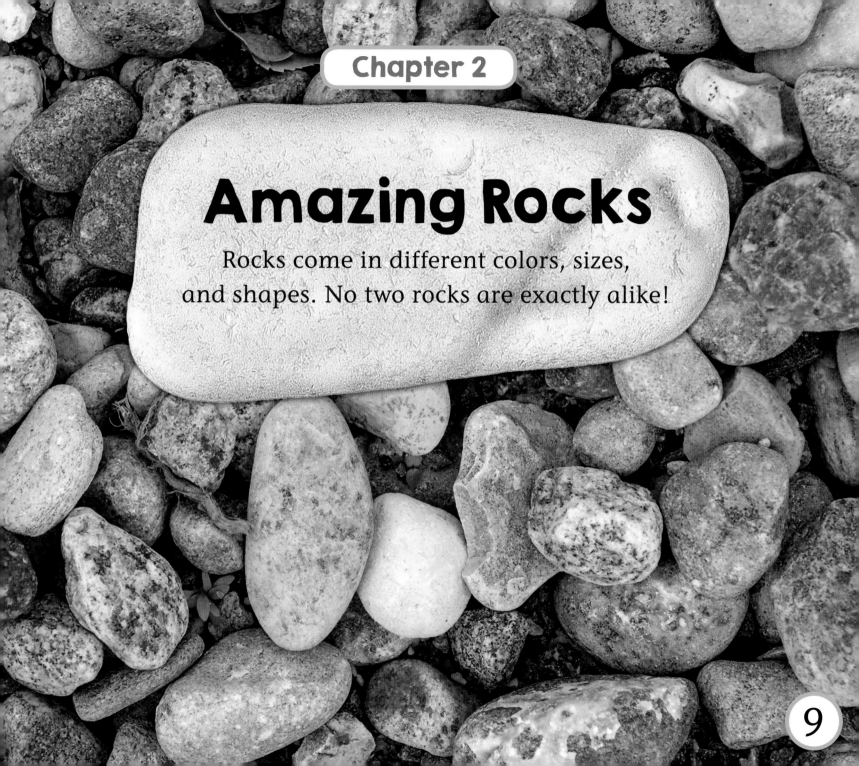

Chapter 2

Amazing Rocks

Rocks come in different colors, sizes, and shapes. No two rocks are exactly alike!

Rocks can be colorful.

Kinds of Minerals

turquoise

bornite

carnelian

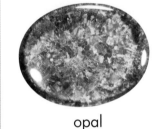
opal

rose quartz

malachite

Rocks are made mostly of **minerals**. Some rocks are made of just one mineral, but most rocks are a mixture of different minerals. Minerals give rocks color and texture.

When you look at a rock under a microscop you can see all the colorful minerals inside

10

Rocks can be sparkly.

Geodes are hollow rocks with sparkly [cry]stals inside. The crystals form when [mi]neral-rich water seeps into the rock. [Th]e water evaporates, but the minerals [sta]y inside. Over thousands of years, [the]se sparkly surprises are formed!

crystals

Rocks can be big.

Can you guess how the Rocky Mountains got their name? They are definitely rocky—and they're enormous! Many animals live on them. The Rockies are also very tall. Brrr! It's cold up there. Sometimes it snows in the summer!

snow

mountain goats

Rocks can be tiny.

Have you ever played with sand? Believe it or not, you were playing with rocks! When wind and water wear away bigger rocks, those rocks eventually get ground down into tiny grains of sand.

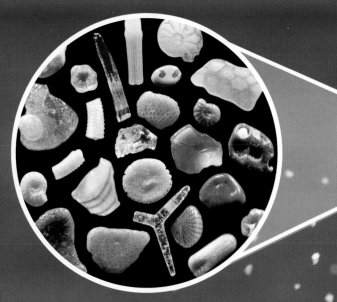

Some kinds of sand have bits of seashells too. Every grain is different!

Rocks can be shapes.

When you look at a rock, it may seem like not much is going on. But rocks are always changing! Wind and water wear away parts of the rock over many years. This can can leave shapes in the rock!

What shape do you see in this rock?

Rocks can be art.

Some rocks are carved into shapes by nature. Others are carved into shapes by people! Artists slowly break off parts of a rock to make a sculpture. This famous sculpture was carved right into a mountain! It shows the faces of four presidents. It is called Mount Rushmore.

This man is checking Abe Lincoln's nose for cracks!

Rocks can be fun!

It's fun to collect rocks. You can find rocks in parks, on beaches, or even in your backyard! Then you can **classify** you rocks by hardness, color, texture, size, or any way you like!

Rocks Classified by Color

pink rocks

tan rocks

gray rocks

black rocks

Chapter 3

Who Uses Rocks?

Rocks can be used in many ways.
They help animals and people get things done!

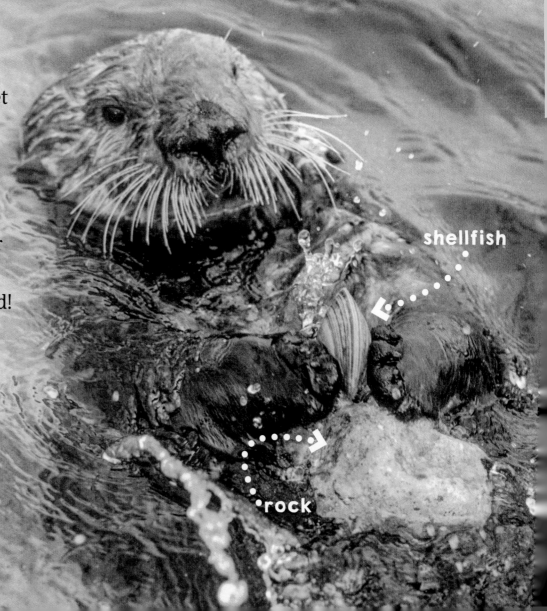 Sea otters use rocks.

Sea otters eat creatures with hard shells, like mussels and clams. So how do they get to the tasty seafood inside?

Sea otters float on their backs and put a rock on their bellies. Then they smash their food on the rock to open the shell. CRACK! Dinner is served!

shellfish

rock

Crocodiles use rocks.

Crocodiles can't chew their food. They
[sw]allow it whole! Some scientists think that's
[wh]y they swallow rocks. The rocks sit in their
[st]omachs and smash against the food,
[wh]ich breaks it up. Smaller pieces of
[fo]od are easier to digest.

Fun Fact

The rocks in a crocodile's stomach
also add extra weight. Some scientists
think this helps crocs dive
deeper and stay
underwater longer!

Chimps use rocks.

Chimpanzees use rocks in a nutty way. They like to eat kola nuts and panda nuts. But the shells are tough to open.

The chimp puts the nut on the ground, picks up a rock, and WHAM! The nut cracks open! It's time for a snack!

We use rocks.

People use rocks too! Did you know you can write with rocks? That's right—chalk is made with rock! And if you're writing on a **concrete** sidewalk, it's made with rocks too!

Did you know there's a rock you can eat? Salt is a mineral that adds flavor to food.

21

Glossary

classify: (**klass**-uh-fye)
To sort by putting similar things into groups

black rocks

gray rocks

pink rocks

geodes: (**jee**-ohdz)
Hollow rocks with mineral crystals insi

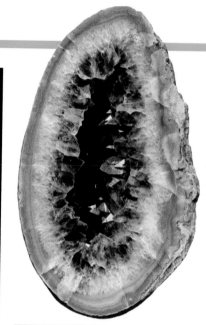

concrete: (**kahn**-kreet)
A mixture of water, cement, sand, and rocks, often used to make sidewalks

igneous: (**ihg**-nee-uss)
A kind of rock that forms when magma cools

pumice

magma:
(**mag**-muh)

Hot, melted rock deep inside Earth

magma

rose quartz

minerals:
(**mihn**-uhr-uhlz)

Natural, nonliving materials found on Earth

malachite

turquoise

netamorphic:
et-uh-**mawr**-fik)

kind of rock that has nged from one form another

marble

sedimentary:
(sed-uh-**men**-tuh-ree)

A kind of rock that forms when wind and water break off tiny pieces of big rocks, which pile up in layers and are pressed together

sandstone

(23)

Index

Photographs ©: cover rough amethyst: Pavel Skopets/Shutterstock; cover raw amethyst: J. Palys/Shutterstock; cover sea glass: T-flex/Shutterstock; cover multiple rocks: MarcelClemens/Shutterstoc cover sulphur: Cagla Acikgoz/Shutterstock; cover malachite: Mali lucky/Shutterstock; cover quartz: Sebastian Janicki/Shutterstock; cover gemstone: Nyura/Shutterstock; cover all other images: vv Shutterstock; cover smiley faces and throughout: Giuseppe_R/Shutterstock; back cover: Felix Lipov/Shutterstock; 2 background: OoddySmile Studio/Shutterstock; 3: Anon Imonoto/Shutterstock; 4 Yongyut Kumsri/Shutterstock; 5 left: www.sandatlas.org/Shutterstock; 5 center: Science Stock Photography/Science Source; 5 right: Harry Taylor/Dorling Kindersley/Science Source; 6 main: shayes E+/Getty Images; 6 top left: Gyvafoto/Shutterstock; 6 inset left: AquaColor/iStockphoto; 6 inset right: Sakdinon Kadchiangsaen/Shutterstock; 7: thoron/Shutterstock; 8 right: Vaughan Fleming/ Science Source; 8 inset top left: Joyce Photographics/Science Source; 8 inset top right: vvoe/Shutterstock; 8 inset bottom left: Tycson1/Shutterstock; 8 inset bottom right: vvoe/Shutterstock; 9: Jarosl Grudzinski/Shutterstock; 10 inset top left: vvoe/Shutterstock; 10 inset top right: David Wingate/Shutterstock; 10 inset center left: vvoe/Shutterstock; 10 inset center right: Jerome Wexler/Science Sou 10 inset bottom left: optimarc/Shutterstock; 10 inset bottom right: TomekD76/iStockphoto; 10 center: Bragin Alexey/Shutterstock; 10 right: J M Barres/age fotostock; 11: Michal Zduniak/Shutterst 12: Andrey Podkorytov/Alamy Images; 13 main: Westend61/Getty Images; 13 inset: www.sandgrains.com; 14: Felix Lipov/Shutterstock; 15 main: Jess Kraft/Shutterstock; 15 inset: Bettmann/Get Images; 16 left: ktaylorg/iStockphoto; 16 right box: Andrey_Kuzmin/Shutterstock; 16 inset top left: maulana ichsan/Shutterstock; 16 inset top right: Ivan Smuk/Shutterstock; 16 inset bottom lef williv/iStockphoto; 16 inset bottom right: enter89/iStockphoto; 16 masking tape: CHALN_CHAI/Shutterstock; 17: Pete Oxford/Minden Pictures; 18: Tome & Pat Leeson/Mary Evans Picture Librar age fotostock; 19 main: Helmut Corneli/Alamy Images; 19 inset: xpixel/Shutterstock; 20: Cyril Ruoso/Minden Pictures; 21 main: Jodie Griggs/The Image Bank/Getty Images; 21 inset: VasiliyBuda Shutterstock; 22 top right: Albert Russ/Shutterstock; 22 bottom left: Alison Hancock/Shutterstock; 22 bottom right: AquaColor/iStockphoto; 22 top left pink rocks: maulana ichsan/Shutterstock; 2 top left grey rocks: williv/iStockphoto; 22 top left black rocks: enter89/iStockphoto; 23 top left: MicroOne/Shutterstock; 23 bottom right: Swapan Photography/Shutterstock; 23 bottom left: vvoe, Shutterstock; 23 top right rose quartz: optimarc/Shutterstock; 23 top right malachite: TomekD76/iStockphoto; 23 top right turquoise: vvoe/Shutterstock.

Library of Congress Cataloging-in-Publication Data

Names: Chanko, Pamela, 1968- author.
Title: The rock book / by Pamela Chanko.
Description: North Mankato, MN : Children's Press an imprint of Scholastic Inc., 2019. | Series: Side by side | Includes index.
Identifiers: LCCN 2018029941| ISBN 9780531131107 (library binding) | ISBN 9780531136485 (pbk.)
Subjects: LCSH: Rocks--Juvenile literature.
Classification: LCC QE432.2 .C464 2019 | DDC 552--dc23

Brought to you by the editors of Let's Find Out®. Original Design by Joan Michael and Judith E. Christ for Scholastic Inc.

1 2 3 4 5 6 7 8 9 10 R 28 27 26 25 24 23 22 21 20 19